This book belongs to:

____

Made in the USA
Columbia, SC
21 November 2022

71833976R00067